LEVEL
1

Pyramids

Laura Marsh

NATIONAL GEOGRAPHIC

Washington, D.C.

For young explorers everywhere —L.F.M.

Library of Congress Cataloging-in-Publication Data

Names: Marsh, Laura F., author.
Title: Pyramids / Laura Marsh.
Other titles: National Geographic kids readers. Level 1.
Description: Washington, DC : National Geographic, 2017. | Series: National Geographic readers. Level 1
Identifiers: LCCN 2016038839 (print) | LCCN 2016039856 (ebook) | ISBN 9781426326905 (pbk. : alk. paper) | ISBN 9781426326912 (hardcover : alk. paper) | ISBN 9781426326929 (e-book)
Subjects: LCSH: Pyramids--Egypt--Juvenile literature. | Great Pyramid (Egypt)--Juvenile literature. | Pharaohs--Tombs--Juvenile literature. | Egypt--Kings and rulers--Tombs --Juvenile literature.
Classification: LCC DT63 .M29 2017 (print) | LCC DT63 (ebook) | DDC932/.01--dc23
LC record available at lccn.loc.gov/2016038839

The author and publisher gratefully acknowledge the expert content review of this book by Jennifer Houser Wegner, Ph.D., associate curator, Egyptian Section, Penn Museum, and the literacy review of this book by Mariam Jean Dreher, professor of reading education, University of Maryland, College Park.

National Geographic supports K–12 educators with ELA Common Core Resources. Visit natgeoed.org/commoncore for more information.

Printed in China
20/RRDS/1

Table of Contents

Great Pyramids

The pyramids in Giza, Egypt, were built 4,500 years ago.

What is topped with a point,
And reaches way up high?

What is built from stone,
With room for a mummy inside?

A pyramid (PEER-uh-mid)!

Egypt Word

PYRAMID: A triangle shape with four sides and a square base

Big Buildings

Pyramids are found in many places. The most famous pyramids are in Giza (GEE-za), Egypt. They are huge. Long ago, ancient Egyptian (AYN-shunt ee-JIP-shun) rulers were buried inside them.

This is a Maya pyramid in Mexico. There are pyramids in Central America and other places, too.

In Giza, the largest pyramid is called the Great Pyramid.

The Giza Pyramids are made of
stone blocks. Each block weighs
more than a big family car.

One stone block would come up
to the shoulder of most men.

Scientists think it took about 20 years to build the Great Pyramid. Workers may have used ropes and ramps.

Building the pyramids was hard work. Thousands of people moved the blocks into place.

6 COOL FACTS About Pyramids

1 The first pyramid in Egypt was called the Step Pyramid. It was built in Saqqara (SAH-ka-rah) more than 4,600 years ago. Pyramids with smooth sides came later.

The Giza Pyramids had smooth sides when they were built. An outer layer of smooth stone covered the pyramids. Today the outer layer has mostly worn away. **2**

3 It took about 20,000 workers to build the Great Pyramid, the largest pyramid in Giza.

4 The Great Pyramid was built with more than two million stone blocks.

Some stone blocks were brought by boat on the Nile River. But many blocks came from an area near the Great Pyramid.

5

The Eiffel Tower in Paris, France, became the tallest building in the world in 1889. Before that, the Great Pyramid was the tallest.

6

Home in the Afterlife

Ancient Egyptian rulers were called pharaohs (FAIR-ohs). People believed pharaohs lived on after they died. This was called the afterlife.

A pyramid was built for the pharaoh's body. It protected the body for the afterlife.

In this wall painting, Egyptians prepare a body for the afterlife.

It took workers many hours to prepare a pharaoh's tomb.

The pyramid was the pharaoh's tomb (TOOM). People filled it with things the pharaoh would need in the next life.

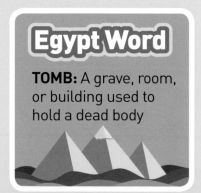

Egypt Word

TOMB: A grave, room, or building used to hold a dead body

Food and furniture were put inside. Jewelry and weapons were put in, too. The tombs held many treasures (TREZH-urs).

These are treasures from a pharaoh's tomb—a hawk, a piece of jewelry, and a painted box.

15

Making Mummies

When a pharaoh died, the body was made into a mummy. Salts, oils, and perfumes were put on the body.

Next the mummy was wrapped with strips of cloth. Then it was put into a coffin.

a mummy

Egypt Word

MUMMY: A dead body that is treated and prepared for burial with strips of cloth

The pharaoh's coffin was often made to look like the person inside.

Inside a Pyramid

A pyramid often had several rooms inside. The pharaoh's coffin was placed in the burial (BEAR-ee-ul) room.

This room was in the middle of the pyramid. A long, narrow tunnel led to it.

More tunnels led to other rooms. Treasures were kept there, too. Some pyramids had burial chambers hidden below the pyramid.

an entrance to a tunnel in the Great Pyramid

Robbers

Long ago, people robbed the pyramids. They dug through the stone. They stole the treasures inside. So pharaohs needed a new kind of tomb. The time of the pyramids was over.

In this illustration, a tomb is discovered. But robbers have already been there.

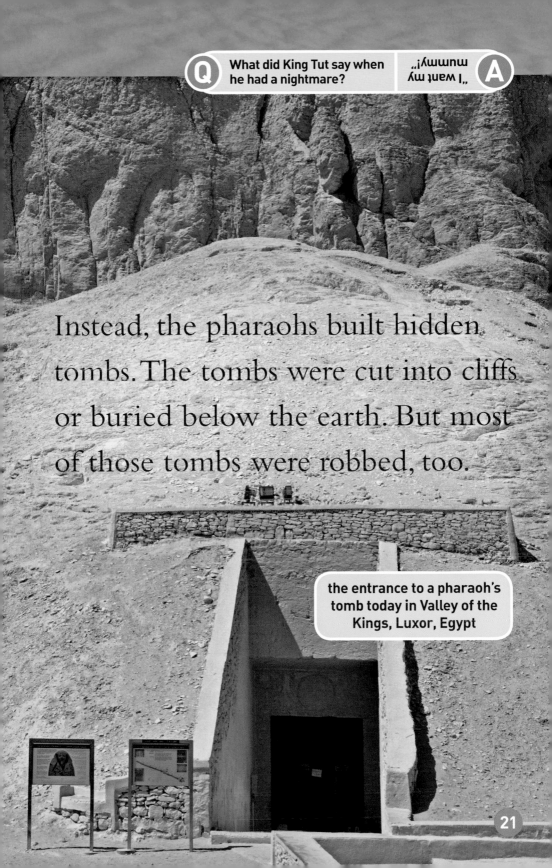

Instead, the pharaohs built hidden tombs. The tombs were cut into cliffs or buried below the earth. But most of those tombs were robbed, too.

the entrance to a pharaoh's tomb today in Valley of the Kings, Luxor, Egypt

King Tut's Tomb

Robbers and explorers found many tombs. By the 1900s, most tombs had been found. But the tomb of one king had not—King Tut.

art showing King Tut and his wife

Howard Carter

A man named Howard Carter
tried to find Tut's tomb.
He searched for many years.

In 1922, Carter found hidden steps to a burial room. Rocks from another tomb had covered it.

Inside was the tomb of King Tut! Carter found a lot of treasures. They were more than 3,000 years old.

Howard Carter studies King Tut's coffin.

This golden mask covered the mummy of King Tut.

Still Exploring

A scientist uses a
machine to scan the
walls in the tomb.

People are still exploring pyramids and tombs. In 2015, scientists said there might be hidden rooms in Tut's tomb! They used new radar scans to find them.

They thought the tomb of Queen Nefertiti (NEF–er–TEE–tee) might be inside!

Queen Nefertiti was the famous wife of King Tut's father.

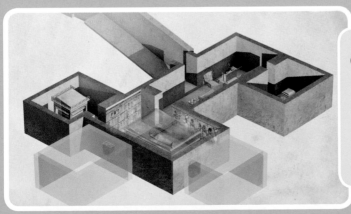

This computer drawing shows a map of King Tut's tomb. The rooms in shadows are possible rooms not yet discovered.

Many more lost tombs and pyramids are buried in the ground. Sarah Parcak has a new way to find them.

Sarah Parcak is at work in the field.

Parcak studies a satellite photo.

She looks at satellite (SAT-uh-lite) photos of Earth. They show where things may be under the ground. She has found hundreds of places to search. Maybe she will find new tombs and pyramids to explore!

Egypt Word

SATELLITE: A spacecraft that gathers information

What in the World?

These pictures show up-close views of things having to do with pyramids. Use the hints to figure out what's in the pictures. Answers are on page 31.

1

HINT: a body wrapped in cloth

2

HINT: Pyramids are built with these.

Word Bank

satellite   tunnel   pharaoh   **Great Pyramid**   mummy   stone blocks

3

HINT: an Egyptian ruler

4

HINT: a long, narrow path inside a pyramid

5

HINT: Sarah Parcak uses these kinds of photos.

6

HINT: the largest Giza Pyramid

Answers: 1. mummy, 2. stone blocks, 3. pharaoh, 4. tunnel, 5. satellite, 6. Great Pyramid

MUMMY: A dead body that is treated and prepared for burial with strips of cloth

PYRAMID: A triangle shape with four sides and a square base

SATELLITE: A spacecraft that gathers information

TOMB: A grave, room, or building used to hold a dead body

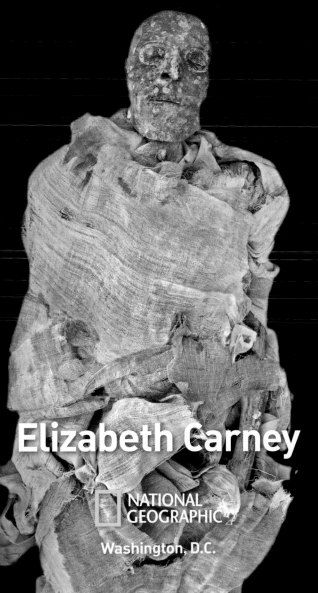

LEVEL 2

Mummies

Elizabeth Carney

NATIONAL GEOGRAPHIC

Washington, D.C.

For Patrick, Brendan, Brian, and Nora. Unlike mummies, laughing with you never gets old.—E.C.

Library of Congress Cataloging-in-Publication Data

Carney, Elizabeth, 1981-
Mummies / by Elizabeth Carney.
p. cm.
ISBN 978-1-4263-0528-3 (pbk. : alk. paper) -- ISBN 978-1-4263-0529-0 (library binding : alk. paper)
1. Mummies--Juvenile literature. I. Title.
GN293.C37 2009
393'.3--dc22
2009003630

**National Geographic supports K–12 educators with ELA Common Core Resources.
Visit natgeoed.org/commoncore for more information.**

Table of Contents

Whoa, Mummy!

A farmer is working in
swampy land. His shovel hits
something hard. He uncovers
a blackened body.

It has hair, teeth, even fingerprints.
The farmer calls the police.
It looks like the person died recently.
But the body is over two thousand
years old! It's a mummy!

The Grauballe Man, found in a swampy bog

Mummy Making

When something dies, it decays. Insects, wild animals, and bacteria eat parts of the body.

A mummy is a dead body that doesn't decay.

A mummy can be made in two ways.

People can use bacteria-killing chemicals to make mummies.

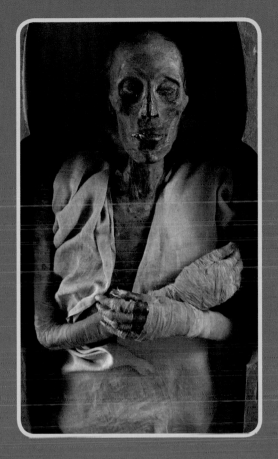

Or, if a body is in the right place at the right time, it can also become a mummy naturally. In those places, any dead body might become a mummy!

BACTERIA: Tiny living things that can only be seen through a microscope.

DECAY: To rot or break down.

Natural Mummies

A bog mummy known as
the Lindow Man

Body-eating bacteria do not grow well in places that are very cold. Or in places that are hot and dry. Or in places called bogs. People have found mummies on frosty mountaintops and in hot deserts.

Bogs are wet, swamp-like places. Bog mummies can be so well kept that scientists could tell one ancient man used hair gel!

BOGS: Swampy areas where special mosses grow. The plants make the area a tough place for bacteria to live.

9

The man's face looks like he's sleeping. But he didn't die peacefully.

This bog mummy in Denmark was found with a rope around his neck. Experts think the man was killed as part of a religious ceremony.

The bits of his last meal, vegetable soup eaten 2,300 years ago, are still in his stomach.

Tollund Man

Ötzi Man

In 1991, two hikers found a man frozen in the mountains between Italy and Austria. A 5,300-year-old murder mystery! The mummy, nicknamed Ötzi (OOT-zee), is one of the oldest mummies ever found.

He wears a cape and leather shoes. But when scientists took a closer look at Ötzi's body, they found a surprise. A stone arrowhead was stuck in his shoulder. Ötzi had been shot in the back! Who killed Ötzi over five thousand years ago and why? So far the case has gone cold!

Ötzi as he might have looked

Man-made Mummies

For thousands of years, people have made mummies. Many cultures believed that a person's spirit lives on after death.

Word Wrap

CULTURE: A group of people who share beliefs and customs

They thought spirits might need things in the next life. That's why mummies were sometimes buried with weapons, jewelry, food, or even mummies of favorite pets.

Different cultures had their own ways of making mummies. Some dried the bodies with sand or smoke. Others used chemicals to preserve bodies.

15

The first people to make mummies
may have been the Chinchorros.

Their mummies are 7,000 years old!
They are the oldest man–made
mummies ever found.

The Chinchorros
mummified everyone
who died, from babies
to the oldest adults. They
covered their mummies'
faces with clay masks.
Then the mummies were
painted to make them
black and shiny.

The culture disappeared
around 3,000 years
ago. These strange
mummies were all that
was left behind.

**MUMMIFY: To treat
a dead body so that it
doesn't break down**

How to Make a Mummy

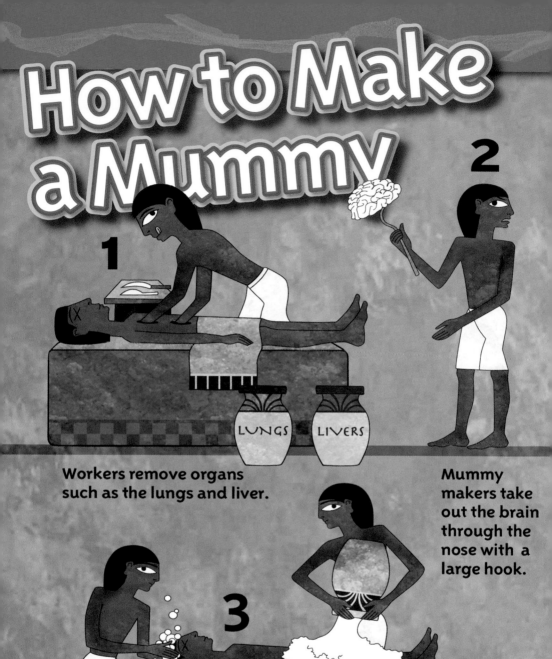

1 Workers remove organs such as the lungs and liver.

LUNGS LIVERS

2 Mummy makers take out the brain through the nose with a large hook.

3 Workers wash the body and cover it with salts.

4

The body is left to dry for 40 days.

5

Workers rub scented oils on the mummy.

6

Workers wrap the mummy in linen.

Tomb of Treasures

Ancient Egyptians made millions of mummies. In 1922, a scientist named Howard Carter found a special mummy in Egypt. Carter peeked into a dark tomb and was struck with amazement. Gold sparkled everywhere.

Carter had found the tomb of Tutankhamun (toot-an-KAHM-uhn)! Known as King Tut, he died over 3,300 years ago. He was only 18 years old. But the young king was buried with priceless treasures. Tut's tomb made him the most famous mummy in the world.

TOMB: A grave, room, or building for holding a dead body

A Mummy's Curse

Howard Carter in the tomb
of King Tutankhamun

After the discovery of King Tut's tomb, people everywhere wanted to know more about the boy king. But not everything reported about Tut was true.

Shortly after the tomb was opened, one of Tut's discoverers died. Some people said that the boy king put a curse on the tomb.

Animal Wraps

Ancient Egyptians didn't just make human mummies. They made many animal mummies too!

Favorite pets were sometimes mummified and buried with their owners. Egyptians thought cats were very special. Sometimes, when a cat died, the whole family would mourn its death.

Egyptians also made mummies of dogs, crocodiles, monkeys, and birds. These animals were believed to please the gods.

MOURN: To feel or express sorrow or grief

Lovely Lady Mummy

Lady Dai may have looked like this.

Over 2,000 years ago, a wealthy Chinese woman known as Lady Dai died.

Her body was treated with salt. Salt takes water out of the body, which helps to keep it from rotting. The body was wrapped in 20 layers of silk.

Lady Dai was put into a nest of six beautifully painted coffins. Workers buried her at the bottom of a tunnel dug deep in the ground.

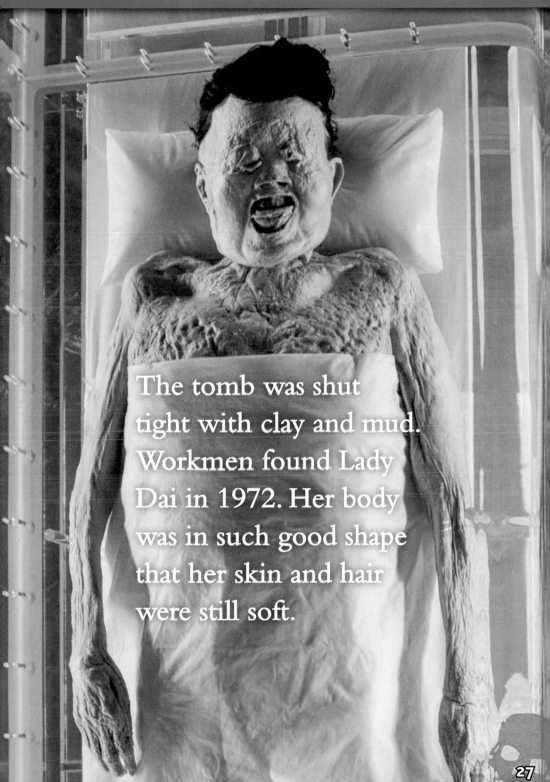

The tomb was shut tight with clay and mud. Workmen found Lady Dai in 1972. Her body was in such good shape that her skin and hair were still soft.

27

Mummies Today

Mummy-making is not just a thing of the ancient past. Some famous people have been mummified since then.

English thinker Jeremy Bentham died in 1832. He wanted his body to be used for science. Students took out his insides. They mummified his head. Then they dressed his skeleton in clothes. You can still go see him in England!

Secrets Unwrapped

Mummies can't talk. But they can still tell us many secrets about the past. Scientists study everything in and around a mummy's body.

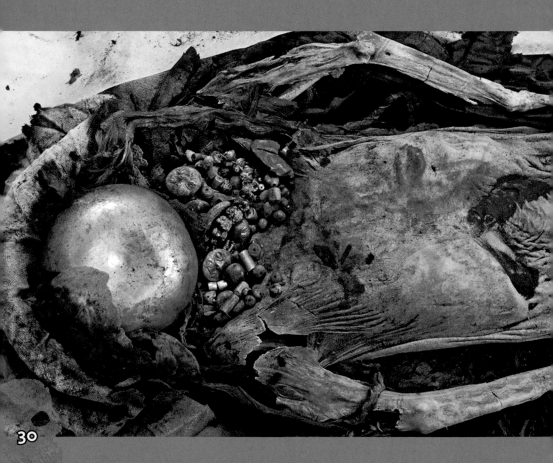

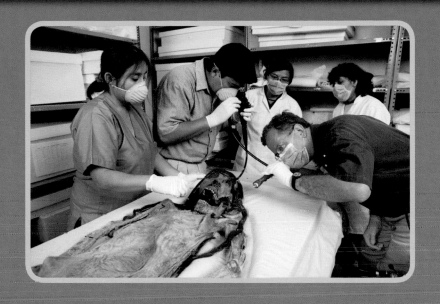

Food left in a mummy's stomach
tells about what people ate.
Broken bones tell about a person's life
and sometimes about his or her death.
Scientists can also examine a mummy's
clothes and the objects buried with it.

All hold clues to peoples'
religions and ways of life. In a way,
mummies are like time machines.

They give us a peek into the past.

DECAY
To rot or break down

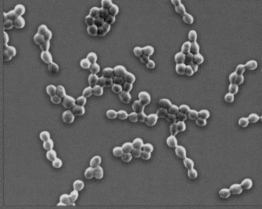

BACTERIA
Tiny living things that can only be seen through a microscope. Bacteria can cause human diseases.

BOGS
Swampy areas where special mosses grow. The plants make the area a tough place for bacteria to live.

TOMB
A grave, room, or building for holding a dead body

MUMMIFY
To treat a dead body so that it doesn't break down

CULTURE
A group of people who share beliefs and customs

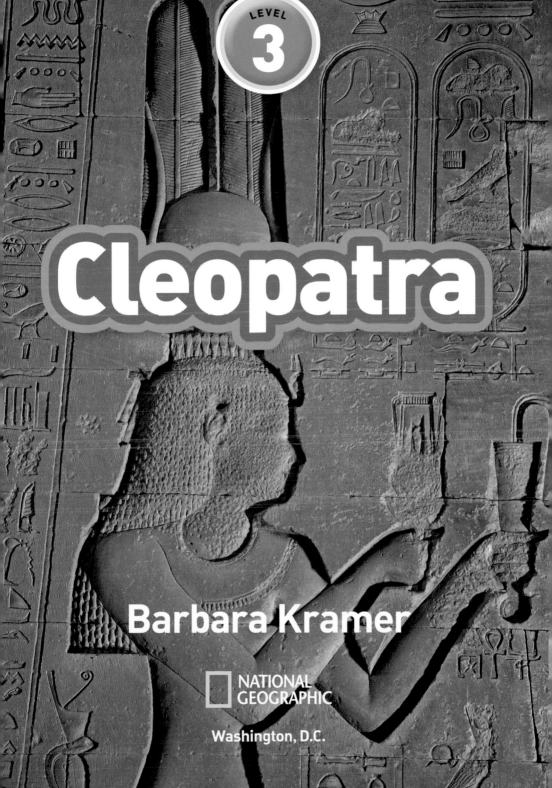

LEVEL
3

Cleopatra

Barbara Kramer

NATIONAL
GEOGRAPHIC

Washington, D.C.

For Kinsey —B.K.

Not much is known about Cleopatra. Myths and legends about her have survived, but how much of them is true is unknown. Much of the early information about Cleopatra came from a book about Mark Antony called *Life of Antony*. The Greek historian Plutarch wrote it more than 100 years after Cleopatra died. Almost all images of Cleopatra's likeness made during her lifetime are gone. The coin with her likeness on page 6 is one of the only images of her that remains. The cover art shows what Cleopatra might have looked like at age 18, at the beginning of her reign as queen of Egypt. Although she was queen of Egypt, current research suggests that she was of Greek heritage, as she is portrayed on the cover. The art throughout this book depicts many different interpretations of Cleopatra.

The lotus flower, featured throughout the book, closes at night and opens during the day. In ancient Egypt, it became a symbol of the sun and creation. The yellow borders at the top of the pages illustrate a type of paper made from the stalks of the papyrus plants that grew wild along the Nile River.

Trade paperback ISBN: 978-1-4263-2137-5
Reinforced library binding ISBN: 978-1-4263-2138-2

Editor: Shelby Alinsky
Art Director: Callie Broaddus
Editorial: Snapdragon Books
Designer: YAY! Design
Photo Editor: Lori Epstein
Production Assistants: Sanjida Rashid and Rachel Kenny
Rights Clearance Specialist: Colm McKeveny
Manufacturing Manager: Rachel Faulise

The author and publisher gratefully acknowledge the expert content review of this book by Jennifer Houser Wegner, Ph.D., associate curator, Egyptian Section, Penn Museum, and the literacy review of this book by Mariam Jean Dreher, professor of reading education, University of Maryland, College Park.

Photo Credits
GI=Getty Images; NGIC=National Geographic Image Collection; SS=Shutterstock
Cover, Patrick Faricy; top border, Jaywarren79/SS; vocabulary box art, Michal812/Dreamstime; 1, Kenneth Garrett/NGIC; 3, Cleopatra VII (69-30 BCE), famous queen of Egypt/Marble bus/:Antikensammlung, Staatliche Museen, Berlin, Germany/Johannes Laurentius/bpk/Art Resource, NY; 4, Photononstop/SuperStock; 5 (UP), Michelangelo Buonarroti (1475-1564) Head of Cleopatra/Casa Buonarroti, Florence, Italy/Scala/Art Resource, NY; 5 (LO), Link, William (19-20th c. Brooch in form of Cleopatra. 1902. Silver. Collection of The Newark Museum/Art Resource, NY; 6 (UP), Kenneth Garrett/NGIC; 6 (LO), Universal History Archive/UIG via GI; 8, Kenneth Garrett/NGIC; 9, Universal History Archive/GI; 10, Christoph Gerigk/NGIC; 11 (UP), The Print Collector/Print Collector/GI; 11 (LO), Sarin Images/The Granger Collection, NYC - All rights reserved; 12 (UP), De Agostini/GI; 12 (LO), Federica Milella/SS; 13 (UP), De Agostini/GI; 13 (CTR), Alistair Duncan/Dorling Kindersley/GI; 13 (LO), Wrangel/Dreamstime; 15, Courtesy Royal Ontario Museum; 17, Cleopatra (69-30 B.C.) before Julius Caesar (100-44 B.C.): engraving after the painting by Jean Leon Gerome/The Granger Collection, NYC - All rights reserved; 19, Sarin Images/The Granger Collection, NYC - All rights reserved; 20, Bettmann/GI; 21, DEA/A. Dagli Orti/De Agostini/GI; 23, Cortona, Pietro da (1596-1669) Caesar Leads Cleopatra Back to the Throne of Egypt./Musee des Beaux-Arts, Lyon, France/RMN-Grand Palais/Art Resource, NY; 25 (LE), George Steinmetz/NGIC; 25 (RT), Late republican denarii with Mark Antony and Augustus Caesa/HIP/Art Resource, NY; 27, Alma-Tadema, Lawrence (1836-1912)/Private Collection/Bridgeman Images; 28, The Banquet of Cleopatra, 1743-1744. Artist: Giovanni Battista Tiepolo/National Gallery of Victoria, Melbourne, Australia/HIP/Art Resource, NY; 29, Bettmann/GI; 30, DEA Picture Library/The Granger Collection, NYC - All rights reserved; 31, ZUMA Press/Alamy Stock Photo; 32 (UP), humihills/SS; 32 (CTR), North Wind Picture Archives; 32 (LO), BlackMac/Adobe Stock; 33 (UP), Bettmann/GI; 33 (CTR LE), sculpies/SS; 33 (CTR RT), Bettmann/GI; 33 (LO), Victoria and Albert Museum, London, Great Britain/V&A Images, London/Art Resource, NY; 35, sculpies/SS; 36, Fine Art Photographic Library/Corbis/Corbis via GI; 38-39, Science History Images/Alamy Stock Photo; 39 (LO), The Granger Collection, NYC - All rights reserved; 40, Batoni, Pompeo (1708-1787): La mort de Marc Antoine l'homme politique et general romain/Musee des Beaux-Arts/Art Resource, NY; 40-43 (border), marina_ua/SS; 41, Baader, Louis-Marie (1828-1920) The Death of Cleopatra/Musee des Beaux-Arts, Rennes, France/RMN-Grand Palais/Art Resource, NY; 43 (UP), Christoph Gerigk © Franck Goddio/Hilti Foundation; 43 (CTR), Christoph Gerigk © Franck Goddio/Hilti Foundation; 43 (LO), Kenneth Garrett/NGIC; 44 (UP), Pakhnyushchy/SS; 44 (CTR), Foley, Margaret (1830-1877) Cleopatra/Smithsonian American Art Museum, Washington, DC, USA/Art Resource, NY; 44 (LO-A), pirtuss/SS; 44 (LO-B), O. Loius Mazzatenta/NGIC; 44 (LO-C), Eugene Sergeev/SS; 44 (LO-D), The sun-boat or funeral boat of Pharaoh Cheops/Giza, Egypt/Erich Lessing/Art Resource, NY; 45 (UP LE), clubfoto/iStockphoto; 45 (UP RT), Patrick Faricy; 45 (LO LE), The Granger Collection, NYC - All rights reserved; 45 (LO RT), Elias H. Debbas II/SS; 46 (UP & CTR LE), Sarin Images/The Granger Collection, NYC - All rights reserved; 46 (CTR RT), NG Maps; 46 (LO LE), Nurse whispering to Phaedra, sarcophagus of Phaedra and Hippolytus/Archaeological Museum Istanbul/The Art Archive/Gianni Dagli Orti/Art Resource, NY; 46 (LO RT), De Agostini/GI; 47 (UP LE), Rue des Archives/The Granger Collection, NYC - All rights reserved; 47 (UP RT), Gaius Julius Caesar Octavianus/Rome, Italy/Album/Art Resource, NY; 47 (CTR LE), Cleopatra (69-30 B.C.) before Julius Caesar (100-44 B.C.): engraving after the painting by Jean Leon Gerome/The Granger Collection, NYC - All rights reserved; 47 (CTR RT), Sarin Images/The Granger Collection, NYC - All rights reserved; 47 (LO LE), Francois Guenet/Art Resource, NY; 47 (LO RT), Prisma/UIG/GI

National Geographic supports K–12 educators with ELA Common Core Resources.
Visit natgeoed.org/commoncore for more information.

Table of Contents

Who Was Cleopatra?

Cleopatra was queen of Egypt more than 2,000 years ago. Today, she is still one of history's most famous queens. Books and plays have been written about her. Movies have been made about her life. Those stories show what writers *think* she was like. The truth is there are many things we do not know about Cleopatra.

Her letters and other writings were lost. Images and statues of her made during her lifetime are gone. They would have offered important clues about what Cleopatra was like. Without them, much of her life is a mystery.

a drawing of Cleopatra by Michelangelo

Elizabeth Taylor starred in the movie *Cleopatra* in 1963.

a modern pin that pictures Cleopatra

A Beauty Queen?

Some people have said Cleopatra was a great beauty. Others said she was pleasant looking but had a hooked nose and a pointed chin. It was the way she talked and acted that made her beautiful. This coin is one of the only images of Cleopatra from her time that has been found.

We do know that Cleopatra was smart, brave, and charming. She was still a teenager when she became queen of Egypt in 51 B.C.

In His Own Words

"The attraction of her person, joining with the charm of her conversation, and the character that attended all she said or did, was something bewitching."
—Plutarch, Greek historian

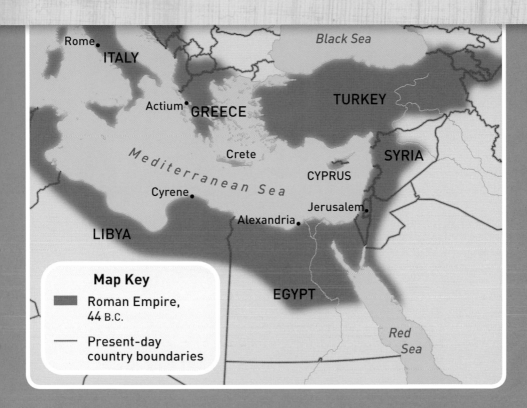

Rome. ITALY

Black Sea

Actium GREECE

TURKEY

Crete

Mediterranean Sea

CYPRUS

SYRIA

Cyrene.

Jerusalem.

Alexandria.

LIBYA

Map Key
Roman Empire, 44 B.C.

Present-day country boundaries

EGYPT

Red Sea

Egypt is in Africa. Its northern border is the Mediterranean (me-di-ter-RAY-nee-an) Sea. To the northwest was Rome. Today, Rome is a city in Italy. In Cleopatra's time, Rome was also the name of a large, powerful empire with a strong army. Roman leaders wanted to control the world. Yet for almost 20 years, Cleopatra kept Rome from taking over Egypt.

Words to Know

EMPIRE: a group of countries or areas under the rule of one government

Birth of a Queen

Cleopatra was born in the city of Alexandria, Egypt, in 69 B.C. Her ancestors, or family from earlier generations, were originally from Greece. But they had ruled Egypt for more than 250 years.

a statue that some believe shows Cleopatra's father, Ptolemy XII

That's a FACT! The calendar we use today began with the year A.D. 1. Cleopatra lived before that time. Her calendar *ended* in the year 1 B.C. On that calendar, the years were counted backward, like negative numbers on a number line, to the year 1 B.C. For example, Cleopatra was born in 69 B.C. She turned five years old in 64 B.C.

detail of a mosaic showing Alexander the Great in battle

Roman Numbers

Historians use Roman numbers as a way to tell Cleopatra's family members apart. In that numbering system, the capital letter I = 1, V = 5, and X = 10. Letters are added together to make larger numbers.

XII = 12
X + I + I = 12
10 + 1 + 1 = 12

A smaller letter placed in front of a large one means to subtract.

XIV = 14
X + (V – I) = 14
10 + (5 –1) = 14

The first person in Cleopatra's family to rule Egypt was named Ptolemy (TAHL-uh-mee). He arrived in Egypt with Alexander the Great, a king from northern Greece. Alexander took over Egypt in 332 B.C. Ptolemy was a general in his army. When Alexander died, Ptolemy became ruler of Egypt. Historians call him Ptolemy I (the first).

Alexandria was a center for learning. Scholars came from all over the world to study there. The city had the largest library in the world. It had thousands of scrolls written in many different languages.

Most girls did not go to school. It was different for Cleopatra. As a member of the ruling family, she got a good education. She studied history, science, medicine, and math. She read the work of important writers. She also learned to speak many languages.

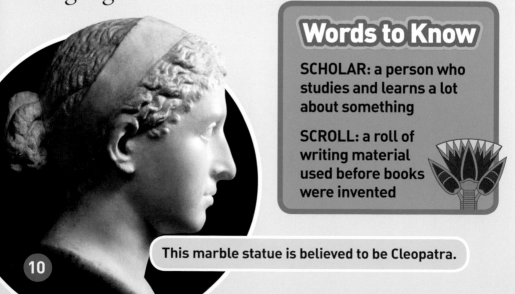

Words to Know

SCHOLAR: a person who studies and learns a lot about something

SCROLL: a roll of writing material used before books were invented

This marble statue is believed to be Cleopatra.

a picture by Harold Oakley of the famous Lighthouse of Alexandria

In His Own Words

"It was a pleasure merely to hear the sound of her voice, with which, like an instrument of many strings, she could pass from one language to another."
—Plutarch, Greek historian

In Her Time

When Cleopatra was a child growing up in Egypt, from about 68 to 52 B.C., life was very different from how it is now.

SCHOOL: Mothers taught their daughters to run a household. Education for boys meant training them for their careers. They usually did the same work as their fathers.

TOYS AND GAMES: Both boys and girls enjoyed playing ball games. They had toy animals and dolls carved from wood or made from clay. They also played board games. A game called senet used a checkered board.

TRANSPORTATION: The easiest way to travel was by boat or barge (barj) on the Nile River. It flowed north to the Mediterranean Sea. Most towns were built along the banks of the Nile.

THE LAND: Each year the Nile River flooded during Egypt's rainy season, from July to October. When the water went down, it left a layer of rich soil for growing fruits, vegetables, and grain.

MUSIC: Guests at parties and banquets were entertained with singing and dancing. Musicians played instruments such as lutes, lyres, and harps.

13

A Fight for Power

Cleopatra's father died in 51 B.C. He left his throne to Cleopatra and her younger brother, known by historians as Ptolemy XIII (the thirteenth). He was only 10 or 11 years old. He was not very interested in ruling a country. That gave Cleopatra freedom to rule the way she wanted.

But Ptolemy XIII's advisers did not want Cleopatra to have so much power. They helped Ptolemy take control of the throne. Cleopatra either left or was forced out of Alexandria. She went to the country of Syria (SEAR-ree-uh). There she raised a small army. By 48 B.C., she was ready to return to Alexandria to fight her brother and his advisers for the throne.

Some believe that this may be a statue of Cleopatra.

That's a FACT!

As queen of Egypt, Cleopatra became Cleopatra VII.

Words to Know

ADVISER: a person who gives advice about what should be done

15

A Sneaky Plan

Luck was on Cleopatra's side. Julius Caesar (JUE-lee-us SEA-zur), a powerful Roman general, had just arrived in Alexandria. He settled into the palace as an unwelcome guest.

Cleopatra wanted Caesar's help to win back the throne. But her brother's soldiers were guarding the palace. To talk to Caesar, she had to get past them.

One night, Cleopatra and a trusted friend sailed into Alexandria. It is not certain how Cleopatra got inside the palace. Legend (LEJ-und) says her friend rolled her up in a rug. Then he carried her into the palace as if the rug were a gift for Caesar.

Words to Know

LEGEND: a story from the past believed by many

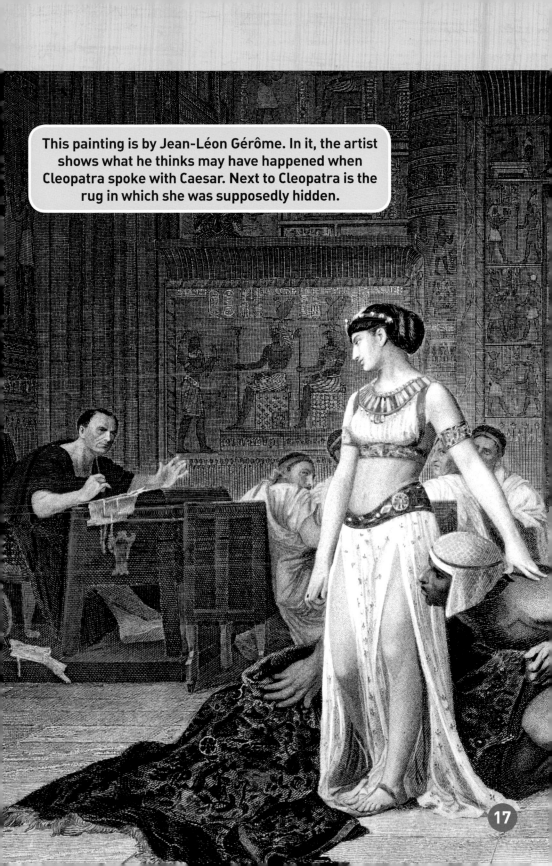

This painting is by Jean-Léon Gérôme. In it, the artist shows what he thinks may have happened when Cleopatra spoke with Caesar. Next to Cleopatra is the rug in which she was supposedly hidden.

Cleopatra had the whole night to talk to Caesar. It did not go as she had hoped. People of that time did not believe a woman should rule a country without a king. Caesar wanted to end the fight between Cleopatra and her brother and make them co-rulers again.

Ptolemy XIII and his advisers did not like that idea. They wanted to get rid of Cleopatra. They could not do that with Caesar helping her. So they went to war against Caesar. After a hard fight, Caesar's soldiers defeated (dee-FEE-ted) Ptolemy's army. Ptolemy drowned in the Nile River.

Words to Know

DEFEAT: to win a victory over someone

CO-RULER: someone who rules together with another

a wood engraving of Julius Caesar from the 19th century

That's a FACT! Caesar was 52 years old and an important general. Cleopatra was only 21, but she was smart. She could also talk easily to everyone she met. Caesar liked those things about her.

A Celebration

a painting of Cleopatra's boat on the Nile by Henri Pierre Picou

Caesar and Cleopatra celebrated their victory with a cruise. They floated down the Nile River in a long, flat boat called a barge. People lined up along the banks of the river to see them. The trip showed the people of Egypt that Cleopatra was queen again.

After a few weeks, Caesar went back to Rome. Before he left, he made Cleopatra a co-ruler with her youngest brother. He was about 12 years old. In history he is known as Ptolemy XIV (the fourteenth).

Queen and Goddess

People from Egypt believed their rulers were gods and goddesses. Cleopatra sometimes dressed to look like Isis, a powerful Egyptian goddess.

a wall painting of Isis from about 1360 B.C.

A Royal Son

In June, 47 B.C., Cleopatra gave birth to a son. She named him Ptolemy Caesar. He was named for Julius Caesar. To historians, he is known as Ptolemy XV (the fifteenth).

Caesar wanted Cleopatra to join him in Rome. A year later, in 46 B.C., she arrived with her son and her brother Ptolemy XIV. The Roman people did not welcome them. After all, Cleopatra was a queen from another country.

Rumors spread. People said Caesar planned to make himself king of the empire of Rome. Cleopatra would be his queen. But Caesar already had a wife. People also feared that Alexandria would replace the city of Rome as the empire's capital.

This painting from the 1600s of Caesar and Cleopatra is by Pietro da Cortona.

A Change in Power

Members of the Roman Senate then turned against Caesar. They stabbed him to death at a meeting on March 15, 44 B.C.

Cleopatra was no longer safe in Rome. She left the country with her son and her brother. Soon after they returned to Egypt, her brother disappeared. It is not clear what happened to him. Cleopatra made her three-year-old son her co-ruler. Once again, she was in control.

That's a FACT!

On the Roman calendar, March 15 was known as the Ides of March. Today, a popular saying is: "Beware the Ides of March." It is a warning of danger ahead.

Words to Know

SENATE: the group that made laws in Rome

Cleopatra and her son, Ptolemy Caesar

Mark Antony

Octavian

After Caesar's death, two men rose to power in Rome. They agreed to rule as a team. Mark Antony ruled the eastern part of the empire of Rome. Octavian (ock-TAY-vee-un) ruled the west.

Meeting the Queen

Egypt was a rich nation, and Rome had a strong army. Antony needed money to fight wars to take over new lands. Cleopatra wanted protection for Egypt from other countries. Antony believed they could help each other.

In 41 B.C., he traveled to the city of Tarsus in present-day Turkey. He sent messages asking Cleopatra to meet him there. She did not reply. She made him wait.

a painting of Cleopatra meeting Mark Antony
by Sir Lawrence Alma-Tadema

Finally, she arrived on a barge trimmed with gold. It had purple sails and silver oars. Young women steered the barge and worked the sails' ropes. Young men fanned the queen to keep her cool.

This 1740s painting by Giovanni Battista Tiepolo is called "The Banquet of Cleopatra."

For the next four nights, Antony and Cleopatra feasted. They also talked about how they could help each other. Cleopatra returned to Alexandria, and Antony soon followed.

On Cleopatra's barge, Antony and his friends ate from silver and gold plates and cups that were decorated with jewels. After the meal, Cleopatra sent the plates and cups home with her guests.

Antony and Cleopatra spent more time together. They played games and went hunting and fishing. Some nights they dressed as servants. Then they roamed the streets, knocking on doors and playing tricks on people.

In Rome, some of Antony's friends and family started a war with Octavian. They were defeated, but their actions created problems for Antony. He needed to let Octavian know he had nothing to do with that war.

sculpture of Mark Antony

On Her Own

In 40 B.C., Antony went back to Rome to make up with Octavian. Once again, they agreed to work as a team. To make their deal stronger, Antony married

a statue believed to be of Cleopatra from around 51 to 30 B.C.

Octavian's sister. It was a way for Antony to show that he was loyal to Octavian.

The news of Antony's marriage might have made Cleopatra sad. But she kept busy with the business of being queen. She met with leaders of other countries. She repaired temples and built ships for a stronger navy.

Words to Know

LOYAL: faithful or trusted

Some believe parts of this document were written by Cleopatra.

7 COOL FACTS
About Cleopatra

1 The name Cleopatra means "glory of her father." On this stone tablet, Cleopatra's name is written using hieroglyphs, ancient Egyptian writing.

2 As a girl, Cleopatra had lessons in public speaking. She learned to talk to both small and large groups of people.

3 Cleopatra was the only member of her family who learned to speak the Egyptian language. Other family members spoke only Greek. This photo shows the Egyptian language on part of an old scroll.

4 Legend says Cleopatra wrote about medicine and math and how to use makeup, but those scrolls have not been found.

5 Cleopatra was born more than 2,000 years after Egypt's famous pyramids were built.

6 In about A.D. 1623, William Shakespeare, a famous writer from England, wrote a play called *Antony and Cleopatra*.

7 Cleopatra was the richest woman in the world during her time.

Trouble Ahead

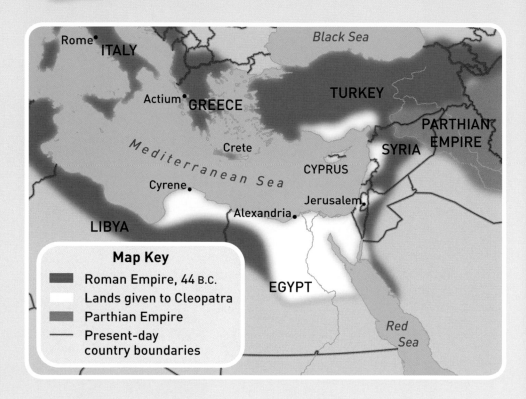

Map Key
- ■ Roman Empire, 44 B.C.
- □ Lands given to Cleopatra
- ■ Parthian Empire
- — Present-day country boundaries

Rome• ITALY
Black Sea
Actium• GREECE
TURKEY
PARTHIAN EMPIRE
Mediterranean Sea
Crete
SYRIA
CYPRUS
Cyrene•
Jerusalem•
Alexandria•
LIBYA
EGYPT
Red Sea

Cleopatra did not see Antony for more than three years. It was business that brought them together again. In 37 B.C., Antony was planning to attack Parthia. That area now includes the countries of Iraq and Iran. Antony needed help from Cleopatra.

She gave Antony ships, soldiers, and money for war. Antony gave Cleopatra some Roman lands in the east. They were areas that had once belonged to Egypt, but they had been lost in wars. Cleopatra wanted those lands to make Egypt strong again.

Cleopatra wanted to make Egypt strong again, as it had been many years before her time.

This detail of an 1866 painting by Alexis van Hamme shows Cleopatra sitting with Antony.

In 36 B.C., Antony went to war against Parthia. He had a large, strong army, but the leaders from Parthia had planned well. They defeated Antony's army.

In Rome, Octavian wanted more power. He tried to turn people against Antony. He said Antony gave away Roman lands to Cleopatra. He also said Antony was under Cleopatra's evil spell. Octavian wanted to go to war against Antony. He knew that was not a good idea, though. Antony still had many friends in Rome. So Octavian declared war on Egypt. He believed Antony would help Cleopatra in that fight. Octavian was right.

"The Battle of Actium" by Neroccio de' Landi

On September 2, 31 B.C., Antony and
Cleopatra met Octavian in a sea battle near
Greece. The Roman ships trapped Antony
and Cleopatra's ships. Cleopatra was able to
break free and Antony followed her. They
sailed to Alexandria knowing Octavian
would follow them. They planned to fight
Octavian on land, but their soldiers gave up.
They did not want to fight the strong
Roman army.

That's a FACT! It was unusual for a woman to go to war, but Cleopatra commanded her own fleet of 60 ships.

Cleopatra made plans to escape. She could begin a new life in another country. Maybe someday she could return to Egypt. That plan fell apart when soldiers burned her ships.

a wood engraving from the 1800s of Cleopatra in the Battle of Actium

39

The Last Queen of Egypt

A story is often told that Antony heard a rumor that Cleopatra had died. He was so upset that he stabbed himself with his sword. Then a messenger brought news. Cleopatra was still alive. Antony was carried to Cleopatra. He died in her arms.

A detail of a painting by Pompeo Batoni from the 1700s. The painting shows Cleopatra holding Mark Antony at his death.

69 B.C.

Cleopatra is born

51 B.C.

Becomes co-ruler with her brother, Ptolemy XIII

49 B.C.

Is forced out of Egypt by her brother and his advisers

This painting called "The Death of Cleopatra" is by Louis-Marie Baader.

No one knows if that story is true. It is also not clear how Cleopatra died. It is likely she took her own life because she did not want to become Octavian's prisoner. One legend says she allowed herself to be bitten by a deadly snake. Others say she took some kind of poison. Historians do know, though, that she died in August in the year 30 B.C.

48 B.C.

Meets Julius Caesar

47 B.C.

Begins her rule with her youngest brother, Ptolemy XIV

Octavian took control of Egypt. Some say he had his soldiers destroy statues and pictures of Cleopatra to get rid of any memories of the powerful queen. Others say those images were destroyed over time by war and nature.

Hundreds of years later, the section of Alexandria where Cleopatra had lived was gone. It was wiped out by earthquakes and flooding. Even now, much of it lies in the Mediterranean Sea. But Cleopatra's legend lives on. More than 2,000 years later, her story is still being told. Yet much of her life remains a mystery.

44 B.C.

Julius Caesar is killed

41 B.C.

Meets Mark Antony

37 B.C.

Gets back lands that once belonged to Egypt

42

Archaeologists off the coast of Alexandria uncover marble statue parts.

An archaeologist searches for Cleopatra's tomb in the Osiris Temple ruins.

The top of a granite colossus is brought to the water's surface in Aboukir Bay.

31 B.C.

Is defeated by Octavian in a sea battle

30 B.C.

Dies in August

QUIZ WHIZ

How much do you know about Cleopatra? After reading this book, probably a lot! Take this quiz and find out.

Answers are at the bottom of page 45.

Cleopatra was born in
_____.

A. Greece
B. Syria
C. Egypt
D. Rome

One thing we know about Cleopatra is _____.

A. how she looked
B. that she liked movies
C. that she liked to dance
D. that she was smart

A barge is a _____.

A. musical instrument
B. game played in Egypt
C. roll of paper for writing
D. long, flat boat

4

In 48 B.C., _____ helped Cleopatra win back the throne from her brother Ptolemy XIII.

A. Ptolemy XII
B. Julius Caesar
C. Octavian
D. Alexander the Great

The name Cleopatra means _____.

A. glory of her father
B. queen of Egypt
C. leader of a nation
D. bright star

5

6

In 32 B.C., Octavian declared war on _____.

A. Mark Antony
B. Egypt
C. Syria
D. Alexander the Great

Hundreds of years after Cleopatra died, much of the area where she had lived was destroyed by _____.

A. fire
B. high winds
C. earthquakes and flooding
D. war

7

Glossary

ADVISER: a person who gives advice about what should be done

DEFEAT: to win a victory over someone

EMPIRE: a group of countries or areas under the rule of one government

RUMOR: information not proved to be true

SCHOLAR: a person who studies and learns a lot about something

CO-RULER: someone who rules together with another

DECLARE: announce or say

LEGEND: a story from the past believed by many

LOYAL: faithful or trusted

SCROLL: a roll of writing material used before books were invented

SENATE: the group that made laws in Rome

Index

LEVEL
3

Ancient Egypt

Stephanie Warren Drimmer

NATIONAL
GEOGRAPHIC

Washington, D.C.

For Mom, who loves golden treasures and creepy mummies with equal enthusiasm —S.W.D.

Designed by YAY! Design

Library of Congress Cataloging-in-Publication Data
Names: Drimmer, Stephanie Warren, author.
Title: Ancient Egypt / by Stephanie Warren Drimmer.
Description: Washington, DC : National Geographic Kids, [2018] | Series: National Geographic kids readers. Level 3 | Audience: 006-009. |
Identifiers: LCCN 2017038021 (print) | LCCN 2017041000 (ebook) | ISBN 9781426330445 (e-book) | ISBN 9781426330452 (e-book + audio) | ISBN 9781426330421 (pbk.) | ISBN 9781426330438 (hardcover)
Subjects: LCSH: Egypt--Civilization--To 332 B.C.--Juvenile literature.
Classification: LCC DT61 (ebook) | LCC DT61 .D73 2018 (print) | DDC 932/.01--dc23
LC record available at https://lccn.loc .gov/2017038021

The author and publisher gratefully acknowledge the expert content review of this book by Jennifer Houser Wegner, Ph.D., Associate Curator, Egyptian Section, Penn Museum, and the literacy review of this book by Mariam Jean Dreher, Professor of Reading Education, University of Maryland, College Park.

Author's Note
The cover features Tutankhamun's golden face mask and the title page shows the pyramids of Giza in Egypt. The table of contents photo is a painted wooden head of the pharaoh Tutankhamun.

Photo Credits
AL=Alamy Stock Photo; CO=Corbis; GI=Getty Images; NGIC=National Geographic Image Collection; SS=Shutterstock
Cover, Kenneth Garrett/NGIC; top border, Fedor Selivanov/SS; vocabulary box art, Grishankuv/SS; 1, Shotshop GmbH/AL; 3, De Agostini/GI; 4, Hulton-Deutsch Collection/CO/CO via GI; 5, DEA/GI; 6, Space Frontiers/GI; 7, Eye Ubiquitous/UIG via GI; 8-9, Robert W. Nicholson/NGIC; 9, Robert Harding/AL; 10, Torleif Svensson/GI; 11, De Agostini/G. Sioen/GI; 12 (UP), De Agostini/A. Jemolo/GI; 12 (LO), Ramin Talaie/CO via GI; 13, Anton_Ivanov/SS; 14-15, Daily Travel Photos/AL; 16, C.F. Payne/NGIC; 17, Mark Lehner; 18, DEA Picture Library/GI; 19, Petr Bonek/AL; 20-21, Prisma Archivo/AL; 22, J.D. Dallet/age fotostock/AL; 23, Stefano Bianchetti/CO via GI; 24, Kenneth Garrett/NGIC; 25, CM Dixon/Print Collector/GI; 26 (UP), De Agostini/GI; 26 (CTR), Peter Horree/AL; 26 (LO), jsp/SS; 27 (UP), Jules Gervais Courtellemont/NGIC; 27 (CTR), Brian Kinney/SS; 27 (LO), CM Dixon/Print Collector/GI; 28, Ann Ronan Pictures/Print Collector/GI; 29 (UP), Ann Ronan Pictures/Print Collector/GI; 29 (LO), De Agostini/GI; 30, De Agostini/GI; 31 (UP), SSPL/GI; 31 (LO LE), SSPL/GI; 31 (LO RT), Werner Forman/Universal Images/GI; 32, Christophel Fine Art/UIG via GI; 33, David Degner/GI; 34, DEA/G. Dagli Orti/De Agostini/GI; 35 (UP), S. Vannini/De Agostini/GI; 35 (CTR), Heritage Image Partnership Ltd/AL; 35 (LO), Werner Forman/Universal Images Group/GI; 36, William West/AFP/GI; 37, Werner Forman/Universal Images Group/GI; 38, Universal History Archive/UIG via GI; 39 (inset), Bettmann/GI; 39, DEA/G. Dagli Orti/De Agostini/GI; 40, courtesy DigitalGlobe and Sarah Parcak; 40 (inset), Mark Thiessen/NGIC; 42, De Agostini/GI; 42-43, Art Kowalsky/AL; 44 (UP), Apic/GI; 44 (CTR), bumihills/SS; 44 (LO), Khaled Desouki/AFP/GI; 45 (UP LE), Dan Breckwoldt/SS; 45 (UP RT), DEA/G. Dagli Orti/De Agostini/GI; 45 (LO LE), Universal History Archive/UIG via GI; 45 (LO RT), Werner Forman/Universal Images Group/GI; 46 (UP), Hulton-Deutsch Collection/CO/CO via GI; 46 (CTR LE), De Agostini/GI; 46 (CTR RT), Patrick Landmann/GI; 46 (LO LE), Stefano Bianchetti/CO via GI; 46 (LO RT), Fotografiche/SS; 47 (UP LE), J.D. Dallet/age fotostock/AL; 47 (UP RT), Ramin Talaie/CO via GI; 47 (CTR LE), Mark Lehner; 47 (CTR RT), Federico Rostagno/SS; 47 (LO LE), courtesy DigitalGlobe and Sarah Parcak; 47 (LO RT), photoDISC

Table of Contents

Peek Into the Past

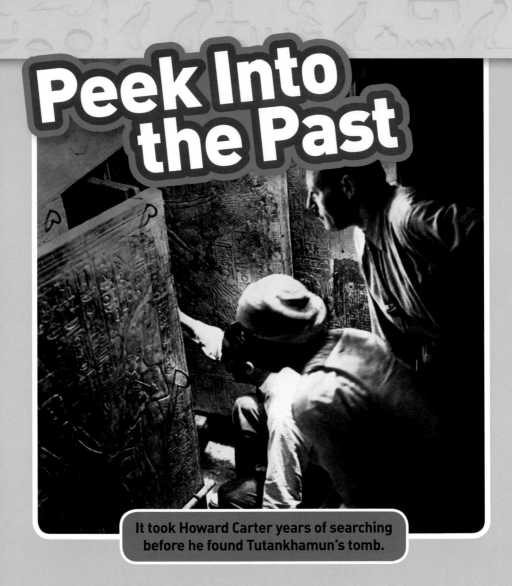

It took Howard Carter years of searching before he found Tutankhamun's tomb.

On November 26, 1922, archaeologist (AR-kee-OL-uh-jist) Howard Carter stood in front of a sealed door. It had been closed for 3,000 years. His hands shaking, Carter chipped a hole in the door and peered inside.

Q What did the little Egyptian say when he woke up from a nightmare?

A "I want my mummy!"

"Can you see anything?" asked a member of his team.

"Yes," said Carter. "Wonderful things."

Carter had found the tomb of the king Tutankhamun (TOOT-ank-HA-mun). It sparkled with treasures. The discovery gave people a glimpse of one of the greatest civilizations in history: ancient Egypt.

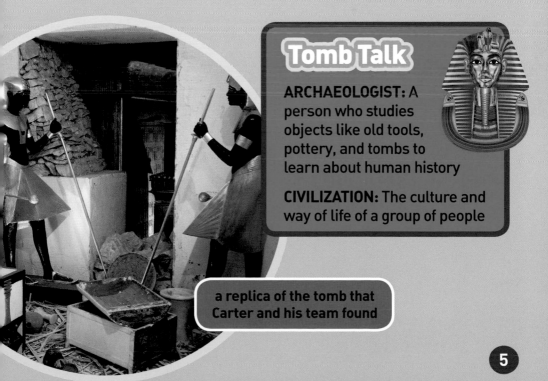

Tomb Talk

ARCHAEOLOGIST: A person who studies objects like old tools, pottery, and tombs to learn about human history

CIVILIZATION: The culture and way of life of a group of people

a replica of the tomb that Carter and his team found

Gift of the Nile

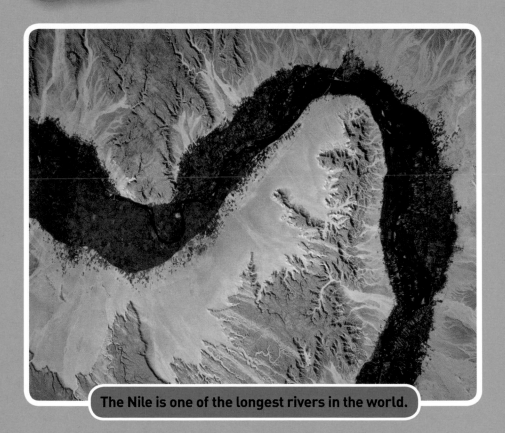

The Nile is one of the longest rivers in the world.

Egypt is a hot, dry desert. But the Nile River runs right through it. The Nile used to flood every year. The flood water left behind thick soil called silt. The silt was good for growing crops.

People settled along the Nile more than 7,500 years ago. To keep track of when they should plant crops, they made a calendar based on the Nile's yearly flood. It had a year of 365 days divided into 12 months. We still use this calendar today.

The banks of the Nile River are green with plants and trees. Just beyond it, the desert land is dry and sandy.

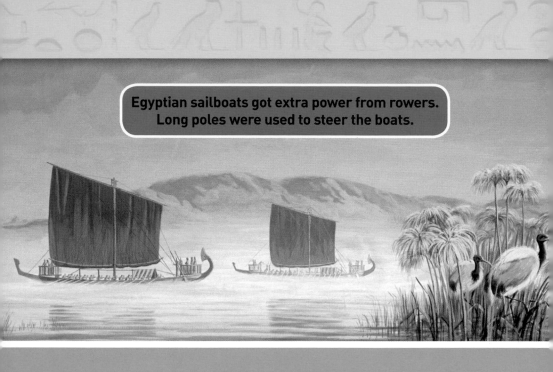

Egyptian sailboats got extra power from rowers. Long poles were used to steer the boats.

Egyptians used the Nile like a highway through their land. They built boats and steered them up and down the river. The boats carried things to trade with other countries.

Ancient Egypt grew into a powerful civilization. It was one of the most powerful in the history of the world. It lasted for nearly 3,000 years, from 3150 B.C. to 30 B.C.

Date Details

The year A.D. 1 is the first year in the calendar we use today. The time of ancient Egypt was before that. Historians decided to count the time before the year A.D. 1 by counting backward from that year. They called those years B.C. For example, King Tutankhamun was born in 1341 B.C. He became king in 1332 B.C., when he was nine years old.

A.D. calendar we use today

B.C.

A.D. 2500
A.D. 2000
A.D. 1500
A.D. 1000
A.D. 500
Year 1
500 B.C.
1000 B.C.
1500 B.C.
2000 B.C.
2500 B.C.
3000 B.C.
3500 B.C.

It's Good to Be King

a statue of the pharaoh Ramses (RAM-seez) II

The rulers of ancient Egypt were called pharaohs (FAIR-ohs). People believed the pharaoh was a god on Earth.

The pharaoh had all of the power. He or she made the laws. The pharaoh owned the land and everything in it.

Artists carved and painted pharaohs onto statues and buildings. They always made the pharaoh appear young and fit—no matter how he or she looked in real life!

This stone carving shows a pharaoh with a god.

Ramses II was one of ancient Egypt's most important pharaohs. He ruled for 65 years and built more monuments than any king before him.

Tutankhamun only ruled for 10 years. But he's famous because he was buried with more than 5,000 treasures like thrones, jewelry, a gold coffin, and a chariot.

In Tutankhamun's tomb, a throne and a chariot (CHAIR-ee-uht) were discovered.

Queen of the Nile

Most pharaohs were men—but not all. For a long time, experts didn't know the pharaoh Hatshepsut was a woman. That's because she ordered statues and paintings to show her as a man—with a beard and big muscles!

a statue of Hatshepsut

Tomb Talk

CHARIOT: A two-wheeled vehicle pulled by horses

Mighty Monuments

Some pharaohs ordered huge structures called pyramids to be built. The pyramids honored the pharaohs. One was the Great Pyramid of Khufu (KOO-foo) at Giza. It was the tallest structure in the world for more than 3,800 years. It was 481 feet tall and took 20 years to build.

the Great Sphinx of Giza

The Egyptians created the Great Sphinx (SFINKS) to guard the pyramids. This statue is as tall as the White House. Its paws are bigger than city buses.

Tomb Talk

SPHINX: A made-up creature with a lion's body and a human head. Egyptians carved sphinx statues to guard important areas.

In this painting, thousands of workers build Pharaoh Khafre's pyramid at Giza.

The workers who built the pyramids did not have machines. Experts think they cut stone from quarries into huge blocks. They dragged the blocks to boats and floated them down the Nile. Then, they hauled the blocks up ramps into place on the pyramid.

Lost City

In 1999, an ancient town near the pyramids was discovered. Long ago, this town was home to workers who built the pyramids. The area was bigger than 10 football fields!

People carefully dig up the ancient town.

Tomb Talk

QUARRIES: Areas where rocks are cut from the ground for building projects

17

Life After Death

The pyramids weren't just buildings. They were tombs. A pharaoh was buried in each of the large pyramids. Smaller pyramids nearby held the bodies of family members.

Animals in the Afterlife

Not all mummies were human. Egyptians sometimes made mummies of animals like this cat. Mummies of dogs, hawks, and even crocodiles have been discovered, too.

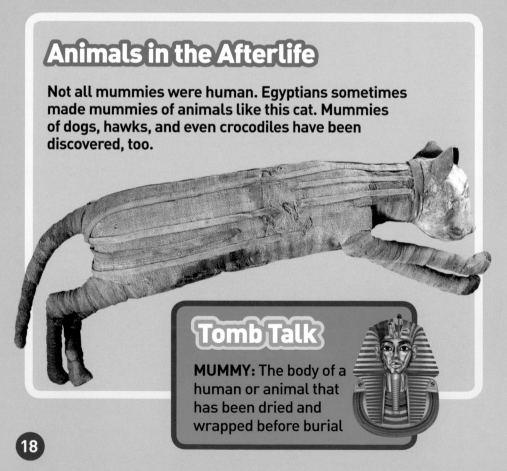

Tomb Talk

MUMMY: The body of a human or animal that has been dried and wrapped before burial

treasures from the tomb of Tutankhamun

Egyptians believed in a life after death. They wanted to make sure their dead relatives would have everything they might need in the afterlife. So they stocked their tombs with things like food, clothes, furniture, and jewelry.

Experts think that the first mummies were made by accident. Egyptians buried their dead in the desert. The hot, dry sand killed bacteria that cause the body to break down. So instead of rotting, the bodies dried out.

This Egyptian mummy now lies in the National Archaeological Museum in Madrid, Spain.

Not everyone was mummified. The process was so expensive that only the wealthy could afford it.

weird but true!

The Egyptians believed that if a person's body was preserved, his or her soul would live forever. They studied these natural mummies. They learned how to make bodies last for centuries. This process is called mummification (MUM-uh-fuh-KAY-shun).

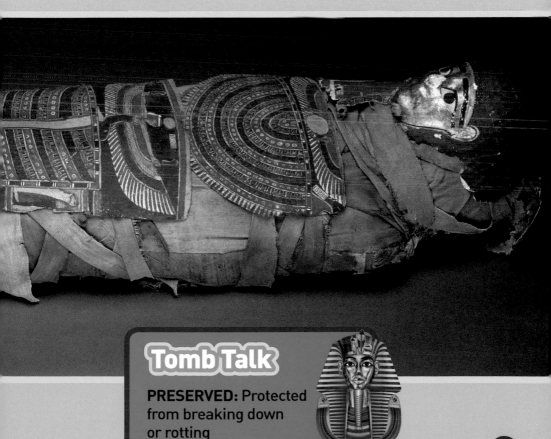

Tomb Talk

PRESERVED: Protected from breaking down or rotting

Making a Mummy

To make a mummy, ancient Egyptians would insert a hook into the dead person's nose, pull out the brain, and throw it away.

Then they removed the liver, stomach, intestines, and lungs. They sealed them in canopic (can-OH-pic) jars. The heart was left in place.

The lids of canopic jars were often decorated with heads.

Tomb Talk

CANOPIC JARS: Special containers ancient Egyptians used to store the organs of the dead

Egyptians didn't think the brain was important. They thought the heart was the source of wisdom.

Next they would pack the body with natron, a type of salt, to soak up moisture. The body was left for 40 days.

Then the natron was removed from the dried body, and the body was filled with rags to shape it. Finally, the body was wrapped in layers of linen.

In this mural from King Tutankhamun's tomb, the god Osiris (left) guides the pharaoh into the next world.

After a person died, the Egyptians believed that he or she would travel to the next world and appear before the god Osiris (oh-SY-riss). He was the judge of the dead.

The person's heart would then be weighed on a golden scale. It was weighed against a feather, called the feather of truth. If the heart weighed less than the feather, the person could live on forever in paradise.

The wolf-headed god Anubis weighs the heart. On the left, the demon Ammut with the crocodile head waits to see if the heart is judged unworthy. If so, he will eat it.

25

6 FUN FACTS About Ancient Egypt

1 The Egyptians thought many animals were connected with the gods, from cats, to cobras, to crocodiles.

Many ancient Egyptians shaved their heads. They did this to keep lice away and stay cool in the heat. They often wore wigs to cover their bald heads.

2

3 The Egyptians grew a lot of grain. Bread and porridge were the main meals of most people.

4

Many mummies wore masks made to look like the faces of the dead. That way the dead person's spirit could find its body again.

Of the seven big, important structures from history called the "wonders of the ancient world," the Great Pyramid is the only one still standing.

5

6

The Egyptians invented makeup. Both men and women wore it. They believed that wearing makeup gave them the protection of the gods.

Life in Ancient Egypt

Gods and goddesses were important in the everyday lives of ancient Egyptians. The Egyptians believed in more than 2,000 of them! They had a god for everything, from daily chores to a safe journey to the afterlife. Each one needed to be worshipped.

Horus was the god of the sky.

This piece of jewelry shows the falcon-headed god, Horus. In each claw, he holds an ankh, the symbol of life.

The god Thoth had the head of an ibis, a type of bird that once lived in Egypt.

Thoth (THOHTH) was the god of writing and science.

Bes (BESS) protected Egyptian families from snakes and scorpions.

The Egyptians thought the god Bes (above) also scared away demons.

Ancient Egyptians thought illness happened when the gods got angry. Doctors used spells to drive away demons. But they had medicine, too. Some didn't work, like an eye cream that included bat blood. But other medicines did. Many medicines included honey, a natural germ-killer.

This painting of a doctor treating a patient's eye is more than 3,000 years old.

Learning From Mummies

From making mummies, the Egyptians learned a lot about how the body worked. Egyptian doctors could stitch wounds, heal broken bones, and perform minor surgeries using blades.

Weird but true!

The first known female doctor was an ancient Egyptian named Peseshet. She practiced medicine when the great pyramids were built, around 2500 B.C.

The temple of Hatshepsut was designed so that the rising winter sun would shine on a statue inside.

The Egyptians weren't just ahead of their time in medicine. They also knew a lot about math. They had to: Their tombs and temples would have toppled without it. They invented a number system based on zeros and ones that is still used to program today's computers.

The sun rises behind the Temple of Karnak in Luxor, Egypt.

They also studied the movement of the sun, moon, and stars. The Great Pyramid's four sides exactly face north, south, east, and west. Many Egyptian temples are aligned along the path of the rising sun.

a boat made of painted wood

Egyptian craftspeople made beautiful paintings, sculptures, jewelry, and furniture. They filled the tombs of loved ones with these treasures. They believed their masterpieces would come to life once the person reached the afterlife.

Art gives us clues about what life was like in ancient Egypt. It shows how people dressed. It also shows what kinds of jobs they had and what they did for fun.

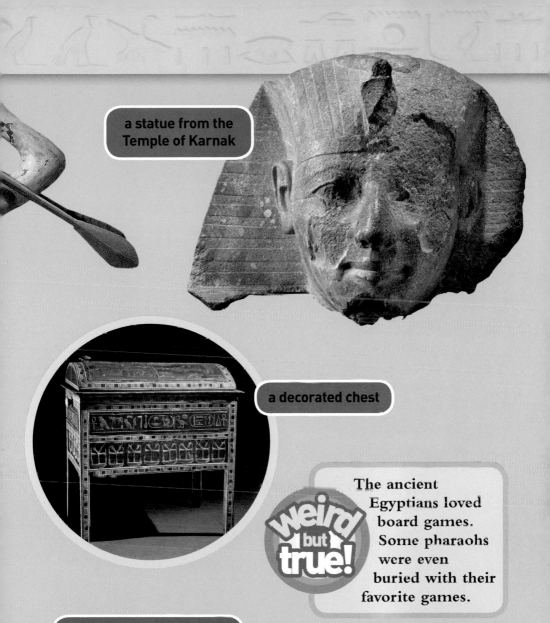

a statue from the Temple of Karnak

a decorated chest

Weird but true!

The ancient Egyptians loved board games. Some pharaohs were even buried with their favorite games.

a popular Egyptian board game called senet

Buried Treasure

Egyptologists (ee-jip-TAH-luh-jists) study art and ancient objects to learn what Egypt was like long ago. They carefully dig up ancient cities and peer inside tombs. They also use modern tools like 3-D scanning. They can find out what's underneath a mummy's wrappings without even taking it out of the coffin!

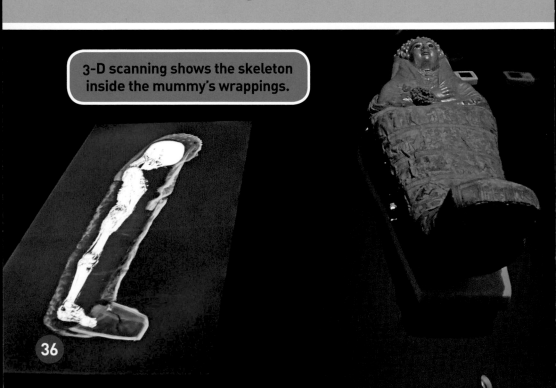

3-D scanning shows the skeleton inside the mummy's wrappings.

Tomb Raiders

Not everyone has treated mummies with such care. Ancient grave robbers broke into tombs. They unwrapped bodies to steal gold and jewels. This happened even though builders made the pyramids with tunnels and empty rooms. They did this to try to trick looters.

Ancient Egyptian police officers used trained dogs—and even monkeys! This carving shows an officer and his trained baboon arresting a thief.

Tomb Talk

EGYPTOLOGIST: Someone who studies ancient Egyptian history, language, literature, religion, architecture, or art

One of the most exciting finds from ancient Egypt happened in 1779. A French soldier discovered a stone covered with ancient writing. It was named the Rosetta Stone. The writing had the same text in three different scripts, or alphabets. One of the scripts was Egyptian hieroglyphs. This language of symbols had been a mystery for 2,000 years. Experts used the other two scripts to decode the hieroglyphs.

the Rosetta Stone

Kamal El Mallakh

Pharaoh Khufu's boat was discovered by Kamal El Mallakh in 1954.

Another big discovery came in 1954. An Egyptian Egyptologist dug up a 144-foot-long ship. It had been buried with the Pharaoh Khufu. It was built to carry the king down the Nile in the afterlife.

Ask an Egyptologist

Sarah Parcak used this satellite image to find the ancient Egyptian city of Tanis.

Sarah Parcak

Sarah Parcak uses satellite images to find lost ancient sites, like pyramids hidden beneath sand and forests.

Q: Why did you become an Egyptologist?
A: I've been in love with Egypt since I was little.

Q: Describe your job in three words.

A: Adventure. Mystery. Beauty.

Q: What's your favorite thing about excavating ancient sites?

A: The team spirit on a dig. It's like family.

Q: If you were an ancient Egyptian, what job would you want?

A: Pharaoh, of course!

Q: What advice do you have for kids who want to be Egyptologists?

A: Study hard in school and read a lot.

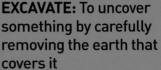

Tomb Talk

SATELLITE IMAGES: Photographs of the Earth or other planets taken by devices in space

EXCAVATE: To uncover something by carefully removing the earth that covers it

Egypt's desert sands still hold many secrets. Whose face is carved on the Sphinx? Where is the famous Queen Nefertiti buried? Egyptologists are looking for answers to these questions—and many more.

This statue is of Queen Nefertiti. She ruled alongside her husband in the mid-1300s B.C.

Does reading about pharaohs, pyramids, and mummies make you want to be an Egyptologist? Maybe someday you'll be the one to solve these mysteries!

QUIZ WHIZ

How much do you know about ancient Egypt? After reading this book, probably a lot! Take this quiz and find out.
Answers are at the bottom of page 45.

What did Howard Carter discover in 1922?

A. the Great Pyramid
B. the Sphinx
C. the tomb of the pharaoh Tutankhamun
D. the Rosetta Stone

1

2

What river flows through Egypt?

A. the Amazon
B. the Nile
C. the Mississippi
D. the Khufu

Who was Hatshepsut?

A. a female pharaoh
B. an Egyptian doctor
C. an archaeologist
D. a male pharaoh

3

The pyramids were _____.

A. temples
B. sculptures
C. tombs
D. grocery stores

What did ancient Egyptians invent?

A. the calendar
B. some rules of math
C. makeup
D. all of the above

What discovery helped Egyptologists decode hieroglyphs?

A. the Sphinx
B. King Tut's tomb
C. the Rosetta Stone
D. the Temple of Khafre

Egyptian doctors could _____.

A. stitch wounds
B. heal broken bones
C. perform minor surgery
D. all of the above

Answers: 1. C; 2. B; 3. A; 4. C; 5. D; 6. C; 7. D

Glossary

ARCHAEOLOGIST: A person who studies objects like old tools, pottery, and tombs to learn about human history

CIVILIZATION: The culture and way of life of a group of people

EGYPTOLOGIST: A person who studies ancient Egyptian history, language, literature, religion, architecture, or art

PRESERVED: Protected from breaking down or rotting

QUARRIES: Areas where rocks are cut from the ground for building projects

CANOPIC JARS: Special containers ancient Egyptians used to store the organs of the dead

CHARIOT: A two-wheeled vehicle pulled by horses

EXCAVATE: To uncover something by carefully removing the earth that covers it

MUMMY: The body of a human or animal that has been dried and wrapped before burial

SATELLITE IMAGES: Photographs of the Earth or other planets taken by devices in space

SPHINX: A made-up creature with a lion's body and a human head. Egyptians carved sphinx statues to guard important areas.

Index